WHY BELIEVE?

Investigate Evidence for Faith

MeLissa Houdmann

Designed and Typeset by Serena Lilli Jeanne

Written by MeLissa Houdmann

ISBN: 978-1-7329889-1-0

Produced and Distributed by:

Stonecroft

10561 Barkley, Suite 500
Overland Park, KS 66212

800.525.8627 / connections@stonecroft.org

stonecroft.org

CONTENTS

DEDICATION

To a special group of Nebraska women whose support enabled us to bring these answers to many more women seeking God and His love.

May loving faithfulness to God's Word be their legacy carried to future generations.

– Stonecroft

WELCOME TO *WHY BELIEVE?*

It doesn't matter where you've been, what you've done, or what has happened to you – God wants to be in relationship with you. And one place He tells you about Himself is in His Word: the Bible. Whether the Bible is familiar or new to you, its content will transform your life and bring answers to your biggest questions.

This study can be done one-on-one or in a group where you can explore together the Christian faith and discover the truth behind God, the Bible, and Jesus. Whatever way you decide to learn, you'll need a guide to help lead you through this exploration.

Every chapter of *Why Believe?* includes a Real Life story of someone who spent time questioning and investigating faith, specifically Christianity, and how it made a difference in his or her life. You'll examine scientific and historical evidence, and discover what the Bible says about each topic. You'll also find a list of more resources if you'd like to explore the topic further.

Thank you for making the effort to find the answers to your questions and examining the evidence. May your journey be fruitful as you come to understand the truth behind experiencing life with God.

CHAPTER 1

God, Are You There?

REAL LIFE – RANDALL NILES

My worldview was simple – attorney and entrepreneur running on the gerbil wheel of life! I spent two decades focusing on personal achievement and material success. I studied business, finance, and law at Georgetown, Oxford, and Berkeley. I worked in glass-towered law firms and high-flying technology companies. To me, life was about self and success.

Based on my intellect and experience, I created my own worldview – my own philosophy for living. Truly, I felt successful and happy. I didn't need a supernatural reason for anything. "Religion" was okay for those who needed a crutch to limp through a difficult life – as long as they didn't limp in my direction.

I believed that all things – from the massive cosmos to the microscopic cell – are the result of unguided natural processes over millions and billions of years. Everything is explained by the physical – there's no need for any notion of the metaphysical. Everything is the result of wonderful chance, held together by chemical-based systems, natural laws, and properties of physics. Smart people with telescopes and microscopes "broke the code" once and for all using 20th century technology. The "facts of science" trump anything philosophical or religious.

Then an inconsequential moment in my life opened a floodgate of far-reaching questions. I needed to look at the observable evidence again. It was time to start examining my decades-old presuppositions about science, nature, and technology. I decided to go back to the big picture basics of the world around me ... I started to read, study, and ask questions."[1]

Around the world, people are asking the same questions about life. They have come to a place where life doesn't make sense anymore and they want to know: "Where did we come from?" "Why are we here?" "Where are we going?" "Is there truth?" Our answers to these critical questions truly affect how we live and interact.

There is one factor that determines the answer to each of these questions and that is a person's belief or disbelief in God. If God exists, we had an origin; we can have meaning and purpose in our lives. If God doesn't exist, where did we originate? Without God, is there meaning or purpose in life?

In this study, we will investigate what we believe and base our conclusions on solid facts. Perhaps you are a seeker who is unsure if God exists. You are wondering why our world is in such desperate straits if there is a loving God out there. You see the scientific facts and you wonder how it all comes together.

Maybe you are certain that God does exist, but wouldn't know where to start if you were called on to share evidence of His existence. This study will present the facts and prepare you to share evidence that backs up why you believe in God.

Each person in the world has a view of God. The basic views can be divided into these categories:

· A theist believes in a personal God who made all.

· A deist believes in an impersonal God who abandoned involvement with His creation.

· A polytheist believes in many gods.

· A pantheist sees an impersonal God who is all – God is literally the universe.

· An agnostic is unsure about God.

· An atheist believes there is no God at all.

Do you consider yourself:

O   **A theist**

O   **A deist**

O   **A polytheist**

O   **A pantheist**

O   **An agnostic**

O   **An atheist**

O   **I'm not sure**

As you consider which of these belief systems fits you, ask yourself these questions: Where did everything come from? Where did time, space, matter, energy, and information come from? If you are a theist, you believe that God created the world and everything in it. If you consider yourself an atheist, you believe that the universe began at some point and you believe in one or more theories or mechanisms of the universe's origin.

So, is there objective evidence of God's existence? Can we know for sure that God exists? Yes – and we can look at science for many of the answers!

Many people believe that science and God are contradictory – that science and theology can't possibly agree. Is this really true? World-renowned physicist Albert Einstein said, "Science without religion is lame; religion without science is blind."[2] Through this study, you will see that God and science do line up in agreement!

Are you willing to have an open mind and look at the evidence? What are objective evidences of the existence of God?

EVIDENCE OF GOD –
If the universe had a beginning, it had a cause.

This evidence for God uses The Law of Causality, which is a fundamental principle of science. This law says, "Everything that had a beginning had a cause."

The question becomes, did the universe have a beginning? Prior to the 20th century, atheists believed that the universe was eternal – it had no beginning, but always existed, with an infinitely long past. Because of Einstein's theory of general relativity, and the many observable evidences that followed, modern scientists now know that the universe had a beginning.

> Science has given us more-than-sufficient evidence that the universe had a beginning and that it erupted out of nothing. This is an accepted fact in modern science. This leaves us with two possibilities: either no one created something from nothing, or someone created something out of nothing. Which option seems more reasonable to you?
>
> O   No one created something from nothing.
>
> O   Someone created something out of nothing.

This evidence of God is very important. Everything that comes to be has a cause. Since the universe is not eternal, but had a beginning, the universe must have had a Beginner.

EVIDENCE OF GOD – Every design has a designer.

The universe has a highly complex design; therefore, the universe had a Designer.

Is the universe highly complex? Absolutely! Take a look around. Since our universe has amazing precision, could it have resulted from an explosion? William Paley gave a great example when he said that every watch requires a watchmaker. Imagine you're taking a walk through a forest near your home. Halfway through your walk you look down and notice a beautiful gold watch lying near a tree stump. Immediately you wonder how it got there. Do you think, *Did the wind and rain come together to form such a beautiful piece of art?*

No, you would never think such a ridiculous thing! You would think something like, I wonder if someone dropped this beautiful watch. You know that the watch was designed by a very talented watchmaker. It didn't result from the wind, rain, erosion, or an explosion. It has clear marks of design. It has a purpose, it conveys information, and it is specifically complex.

The universe is much more precise and awe-inspiring than that watch. The same characteristics we use to recognize design in something like a watch are the characteristics we use to recognize design in nature. When Isaac Newton studied our solar system he said, "This most beautiful system of the sun, planets, and comets could only proceed from the counsel and dominion of an intelligent and powerful Being."[3]

One of the most powerful arguments that the universe has an Intelligent Designer is the anthropic principle, which states that the earth is perfectly designed for life. For instance, if the oxygen concentration in the atmosphere was only slightly lower, human beings would not survive. If oxygen levels were slightly higher, materials would too easily catch fire. If the carbon dioxide levels were slightly higher, Earth would have a super-hot environment like Venus. If they were lower, plants would not be able to survive.[4]

There are also more than 100 precisely defined constants describing the structure of our universe. One is gravity. If the strength of gravitational force were altered by the tiniest fraction (1×10^{-36} or 0.000000000000000 000000000000000000001%), our sun would not exist, and we wouldn't either![5] Other constants, such as the strong nuclear force, weak nuclear force, and electromagnetism have to be exactly balanced, otherwise life anywhere would be impossible.

How big is our universe? Our galaxy alone contains more than 100 billion stars. The average distance between two stars is 30 trillion miles! If you could travel through space at 17,000 miles an hour (as far as man-made spacecraft), it would take you 201,450 years to travel between two stars. It is estimated that the number of stars in our galaxy is equivalent to the number of grains of sand on all the beaches in the world! This universe is indescribable![6]

HISTORICAL FACT: When the first astronauts passed over the surface of the moon and saw the earth, they quoted from the book of Genesis, "In the beginning God created the heavens and the earth." They were overwhelmed by what they saw before them! At the age of 77, space pioneer John Glenn looked out of the space shuttle Discovery and marveled at what he saw.

The vastness of our universe to the tiniest parts of this world brings awesome wonder at the work of God. Our world is filled with creatures that could not have evolved. Consider the bombardier beetle. This particular beetle has a unique defense system – twin exhaust tubes in its tail that allow it to fire boiling gasses at its enemies.

The beetle's body produces and mixes several chemicals that would normally react dangerously to one another. To effectively use them, the beetle requires a complex arrangement of valves and chambers, as well as precise mixing. All these parts need to work perfectly together every time. If all parts had to evolve through trial and error, the bombardier beetle would have blown itself up years ago!

REAL LIFE – RANDALL NILES, CONTINUED

My studies brought me to consider parts of the human body. The human eye is enormously complicated – a perfect and interrelated system of about 40 individual subsystems, including the retina, pupil, iris, cornea, lens, and optic nerve. For instance, the retina has approximately 137 million special cells that respond to light and send messages to the brain. About 130 million of these cells look like rods and handle the black and white vision. The other 7 million are cone-shaped and allow us to see in color. The retina cells receive light impressions, which are translated to electric pulses and sent to the brain via the optic nerve. A special section of the brain called the visual cortex interprets the pulses to color, contrast, depth, etc., which allows us to see "pictures" of our world.

Incredibly, the eye, optic nerve, and visual cortex are totally separate and distinct subsystems. Yet, together, they capture, deliver, and interpret up to 1.5 million pulse messages a millisecond! It would take dozens of super computers programmed perfectly and operating together flawlessly to even get close to performing this task."[7]

As Nobel Prize winning biologist George Wald stated, "The most complex machine man has devised—say an electronic brain—is child's play compared with the simplest of living organisms. The especially trying thing is that complexity here involves such small dimensions. It is on the molecular level; it consists of a detailed fitting of molecule to molecule such as no chemist can attempt."[8]

Do these statistics and accounts give credibility to the fact that an Intelligent Designer created the universe?

Think back over your life. What is the most awe-inspiring view of nature you have ever seen?

Could this unexplainable view of nature be the result of an unexplained explosion, as some people believe, or was the universe crafted by an Intelligent Designer?

Nobel laureate Arno Penzias says, "Astronomy leads us to a unique event, a universe which was created out of nothing and delicately balanced to provide exactly the conditions required to support life. In the absence of an absurdly improbable accident, the observations of modern science seem to suggest an underlying, one might say, supernatural plan."[9]

"Astronomers now find they have painted themselves into a corner because they have proven, by their own methods, that the world began abruptly in an act of creation to which you can trace the seeds of every star, every planet, every living thing in this cosmos and on the earth. And they have found that all those happened as a product of forces they cannot hope to discover. ... That there are what I or anyone would call supernatural forces at work is now, I think, a scientifically proven fact."

– Robert Jastrow[10]

EVIDENCE OF GOD – Every law has a lawgiver.

If we believe there is a moral law, it seems logical that there is a moral lawgiver.

Even the most remote tribes that have been cut off from the rest of civilization observe a moral code. They don't just believe things that "are" or "are not." They believe some things "should be" and some things "should not be" done. Every civilization promotes behavior it believes to be good and/or acceptable, while deeming other behaviors as evil or worthy of punishment. Where then do we get the idea of right and wrong? Perhaps this moral law (or conscience) comes from an ultimate lawgiver above man.

> Moral law is often referred to as the "conscience" or the fundamental sense of right and wrong. Most people have a desire to do the right thing. Where did that conscience come from?

If we believe there is some sort of moral law, then we can assume that there is a lawgiver.

If all the evidence we studied today is true, the obvious next step is to learn who this Creator is. If you are Someone's creature, and subject to Someone's authority, shouldn't you know more about this Creator?

The natural law of Cause and Effect states that an effect is always less than its cause. Since everything – all the matter and energy in this universe – was formed, can we logically assume that the Creator is all-powerful?

Since the combined knowledge that we possess and the past, present, and future knowledge that all mankind possesses came from the Creator, logic tells us that the Creator is all-knowing.

We know the Creator exists outside of our physical dimensions and is not bound by space and time.

Observing the incredible complexity of our universe, does it seem reasonable to presume that the Creator is supremely intelligent?

We know that the Creator must be a personal being because humans are personal beings and have emotions and feelings.

Since the Creator formed morality, can we logically assume that the Creator is absolutely pure and has an unchangeable standard of morality?

If the Creator is all-powerful, all-knowing, transcendent, and personal, what does that say about humans? Surely, we were created for a reason.

With a close look at the characteristics we just mentioned, you will notice that this Creator is consistent with the God of the Bible! These attributes line up perfectly.

Since the Bible is the main source of information about God, let's see what the Bible says about Him. Read the following verses and write what each verse says about God.

Isaiah 44:6 (Page 551)

Psalm 19:1 (Page 421)

Exodus 34:6-7 (Page 71)

Isaiah 6:3 (Page 521)

What does the Bible say about the universe in these verses?

Isaiah 45:18 (Page 553)

Romans 1:20 (Page 857)

THINK IT OVER

If God is the ultimate Designer of the universe, then who made God?

Earlier in the Chapter, we learned about The Law of Causality. It says that everything that "comes to be" needs a cause. God doesn't need a cause since He never had a beginning. He is eternal. This is actually a necessary idea: there must be one single "first" cause to start all other causes. Like the engine on a freight train, there must be one "unmoved" mover to start the process of causality.

If God created the world, why does evil exist? Did God create evil?

This is a question that has plagued many people through the history of mankind. It is important to realize that evil was not created in the sense that a rock or a tree was created. Rather, evil is something that occurs and exists. Evil is the absence of good. For example, consider a plot of dirt that is ready to be planted with vegetables. The gardener digs holes in preparation for planting the seeds. What are those holes? In reality, the holes are just the absence of dirt. In the same way, darkness is the absence of light and cold is the absence of heat. Evil is the absence of good.

When God created the universe, all that existed was good. God gave humans the freedom to choose good. In order for them to choose good, He allowed another choice – evil.

Why does God allow bad things to happen to good people?

Natural disasters kill thousands of people, a father hurts his children, cancer plagues a child. We often ask, "Why do these things happen?"

When God created the first humans, He allowed Adam and Eve the freedom to choose right or wrong. They chose wrong and evil entered the world. Often, bad things happen as a result of evil in the world.

Sometimes bad things happen as a result of someone's bad decision. For example, someone driving drunk kills an innocent person. God's creation of that person did not cause him or her to drive drunk. It was a wrong choice that the driver made.

In our circumstances, remember that God has a greater good, a good bigger than ourselves. As you continue through these chapters, you'll learn about the best Person who ever lived, yet suffered greatly for God's greater good.

No matter what situations we face, we can be certain that God is in control of the ultimate outcome whether we are there to witness it or not. God will bring about a greater good from a desperate situation. Let's see how He worked in our Real Life situation.

REAL LIFE – RANDALL NILES, CONTINUED

My precious mom found herself in a battle with cancer. She had just endured another round of chemotherapy and we sat together and listened to the results. The bottom of my stomach dropped to the floor. In an instant, my detached positivism started to shake at the seams. I listened as we were told about elevated cancer markers and a diminishing list of treatment alternatives. As the oncologist and my mother were talking about the trade-off between ongoing treatment and quality of life, I was trying to get my emotional bearings.

In one instant, my atheism shattered. It was one instant of seeing her pain that the reality of God and the truth about life became real to me. It was at that point in time that I knew God was real. My mind started opening up to all the evidence. I felt very awkward and alone. I was shocked by the truth of my mother's disease and emotional about her uncertain future. It was then and there that I realized I needed to do more than mask feelings with supposed intellect and positivism.

You see, for over 20 years my mom had been praying that something – anything – would reveal God to me and bring me to my knees before God. When I consider why a loving God would allow bad things to happen to good people, I remember one of my mom's last journal entries before she went to heaven. It says, "God does answer prayers in mysterious ways, and does answer a mother's most fervent prayers for the soul of her beloved son. What a grand purpose for my cancer. I agree with Paul in Romans 8, 'For I consider that the sufferings of this present time are not worthy to be compared with the glory which shall be revealed in us.'"

My mom's painful trial was given meaning. As hard as it is for me to understand – I now realize that God lives in the eternal and we live in the now. God looks at what's best in the big picture, while we stumble around in our day-to-day notions of fairness. Sometimes trial and pain actually reflect mercy and love when viewed through the telescope of eternity.

Have you seen God work a seemingly hopeless situation into good?

After seeing this evidence:
- ○ I believe that the God of the Bible exists.
- ○ I don't believe in the God of the Bible.
- ○ I'm still not sure. I have these questions:

Written language is perhaps the most precise medium of communication. It can be duplicated and passed down through the generations. There have been numerous so-called holy books passed down through the years. How do we know which one is relevant and inspired by God Himself?

In the next lesson, we will discover answers to these questions. Is the Bible true? Did it come from God Himself? What evidence is there for its authority and inspiration?

CLOSING PRAYER

Dear God, thank You for creating each of us and the world that we enjoy each day. Thank You for the evidence You give us about Your existence. Help us grow to know You better through this study. Amen.

FOCUS POINTS

EVIDENCE #1 – Since the universe had a beginning, it had a cause.

Science teaches that the universe had a beginning. Since the universe is not eternal, the universe must have a Beginner.

EVIDENCE #2 – Every design has a designer.

The universe has a highly complex design, therefore the universe had an Intelligent Designer.

EVIDENCE #3 – Every law has a lawgiver.

Since there is moral law, there must be a moral lawgiver. Every culture has similar moral laws, giving credence to a Universal Lawgiver.

DIG DEEPER – Evidence of God's Existence

www.AnswersinGenesis.org and www.discovery.org

Norman Geisler and Patty Tunnicliffe, *Reasons for Belief: Easy-to-Understand Answers to 10 Essential Questions*, Bethany House, 2013.

Norman Geisler and Frank Turek, *I Don't Have Enough Faith to Be an Atheist*, Crossway Books, 2004.

Alex McFarland, *10 Answers for Atheists: How to Have an Intelligent Discussion About the Existence of God*, Bethany House, 2012.

Lee Strobel and Jane Vogal, *The Case for a Creator: A Journalist Investigates Scientific Evidence That Points Toward God*, Zondervan, 2004.

Ravi Zacharias, *The End of Reason: A Response to the New Atheists*, Zondervan, 2008.

CHAPTER 2

God, Did You Leave a Message?

So many people wish they could answer their cell phones and receive a message straight from God! Well, the chances of that happening are slim, but many people believe that God has left each of us a personalized message in the Bible.

But how do we know the Bible is true? Is there evidence we can examine to determine whether this book came from God or merely from human hands? Has the Bible been corrupted through the years of transcription? Can the Bible be considered an authoritative source in which to find answers? Is it just a mythical book or something more?

If someone who had never seen a Bible asked you to describe it in a few words, what would you say?

The Bible is a collection of books that is divided into the Old Testament and New Testament. The Old Testament was written in Hebrew with small portions in Aramaic. The books of the New Testament were written entirely in Greek, which was the common language of the people.

Unquestionably, the Bible is the world's best-seller with countless copies in print. But does that make it authoritative?

What are the key evidences for the validity of the Bible?

EVIDENCE OF MANUSCRIPTS – The Bible stands alone as the best-preserved literary work of all history.

It was completed nearly 2,000 years ago, yet over 24,000 ancient New Testament manuscripts have been discovered. No other ancient document begins to approach that many discovered texts. The nearest comparable literary work is Homer's Iliad. That work has less than 2,000 discovered manuscripts.[1] That's a pretty significant difference!

Another key to manuscript evidence is the time span between the date a document is written until the next copied manuscript. The shorter the time span, the better chances for accuracy.

Work	When Written	Earliest Copy	Timespan	Number of Copies
Iliad	900 B.C.	400 B.C.	500 years	less than 2,000
NT*	A.D. 40-100	A.D. 125	85-25 years	over 24,000

*New Testament

F.F. Bruce states, "There is no body of ancient literature in the world which enjoys such a wealth of good textual attestation (evidence) as the New Testament."[2]

HISTORICAL FACT: Before the invention of the printing press, ancient manuscripts were copied by hand. This was a very tedious process and great care was taken by the Jewish scribes through an intricate method for counting letters, words, and paragraphs. Their lives were dedicated to ensuring that no copy errors were made. When one copy error was made, the entire scroll was destroyed. When a manuscript was finished, it was checked and verified to be an exact duplicate. Then the copy was given equal authority as the manuscript from which it was copied.[3]

What about the Old Testament? Between 1947 and 1956, the Dead Sea Scrolls were discovered in 11 caves near the Dead Sea. The scrolls are comprised of animal skins, papyrus, and one is of copper. Fragments of every book of the Old Testament have been discovered, except for the book of Esther. There were remains of about 825 to 870 separate scrolls (40,000 fragments). This discovery was the most significant archaeological discovery of modern times. These scrolls are the oldest of Old Testament manuscripts ever found, dating back to 100-200 B.C.

Manuscript evidence for the Bible far outweighs any other ancient work. Scholars rarely question the authentic nature of other ancient classics – ones by Caesar, Plato, Tacitus, and so on – even though the number of manuscripts found are extremely low and the time span between the date a document is written until the next copied manuscript is much larger than that of the New Testament. Since the discovery of the Dead Sea Scrolls, the Old Testament also has sufficient manuscript evidence to verify its authenticity.

EVIDENCE OF ARCHAEOLOGY –
Archaeological evidence presents compelling support that the Bible is accurate in what it describes.

Numerous excavations over the years have lent credibility to cities and places mentioned in the Bible. Civilizations have been discovered, such as Ur, Huran, Babylon, Jericho, ancient Mesopotamia, Dan, Meggido, and many more!

Many of the people mentioned in the Bible have also been proven through archaeology. For example, the House of David inscription was discovered in 1994. It appears to be a fragment of a victory monument erected by a king during the 8th or 9th century B.C. That's as little as 100 years, and no more than 250 years, after the time of David. The inscription tells of victories over a king of the "House of David." This inscription proves that David was a real person in history, just as the Bible records.

One of the most dramatic finds was a collection of clay tablets and prisms that date to about 2100 B.C. These tablets, collectively named the Sumerian King List, record kings in two categories: those who reigned before the "great flood" and those who reigned after it. The life spans of kings before the flood were much longer, just as the Bible presents.

Evidence has also been discovered to verify the Bible's account of ancient Israel. One example is the Israel Stele (stee-lee).[4] This stone is the earliest extrabiblical reference to the nation of Israel.[5] The stone indicates that at the time of the inscription ("Israel is laid waste, its seed is not") that Israel was significant enough in the late 13th century B.C. to be included on this stone.

An in-depth study of numerous archaeological finds would take several weeks, but if this subject interests you, do further study by using the resources found in the Dig Deeper section at the end of this chapter.

EVIDENCE OF PROPHECY –
The Bible has proven to be completely accurate in the prophecies that have been fulfilled.

A prophecy is a predication of what is to happen in the future. The Bible claims to have 100 percent success in predicting future events. Is this true? Some scholars list over 1,000 biblical prophecies and say that more than two-thirds of them have already been fulfilled. The rest are still capable of being fulfilled. Let's study some of these claims.

Here are two examples. (More can be studied using the resources in Dig Deeper.)

1) Biblical Prophecy:

Isaiah 44:28 proclaims that Cyrus will be the king who will allow the Israelites to return to Jerusalem and rebuild its Temple: "When I say of Cyrus, 'He is my shepherd,' he will certainly do as I say. He will command, 'Rebuild Jerusalem'; he will say, 'Restore the Temple.'" It is important to note that at the time this prophecy was written, there was no king named Cyrus and the temple was still in full operation.

Historical Fulfillment:

More than 100 years later, Nebuchadnezzar, the king of Babylon, destroyed the temple in 586 B.C. Jews living in Jerusalem were killed or taken captive to Babylon. In 539 B.C., the Persians conquered the Babylonian empire. Then Cyrus, a Persian king, declared that the Jews could return to Jerusalem and rebuild their temple.

2) Biblical Prophecy:

Daniel 11:3-4: "Then a mighty king will rise to power who will rule with great authority and accomplish everything he sets out to do. But at the height of his power, his kingdom will be broken apart and divided into four parts. It will not be ruled by the king's descendants, nor will the kingdom hold the authority it once had. For his empire will be uprooted and given to others."

Historical Fulfillment:

Alexander the Great (336-323 B.C.) died at age 32 shortly after conquering the Persian Empire. His empire was not passed on to his children but was divided up among his generals. Four lesser kingdoms emerged from the rubble of Alexander's empire: Greece, Asia Minor, Syria, and Egypt.

There are many prophecies given in the Old Testament that are fulfilled in the New Testament. The prophecies were written hundreds of years before their fulfillments. We will study several of these in the next chapter.

EVIDENCE OF PRESERVATION – Through the years, the Bible has proved to be indestructible.

Even though the oldest parts of the Bible were written nearly 3,000 years ago, the Bible has survived relentless, determined opposition. This fact emphasizes the divine origin of the Bible. Other ancient writings have been lost. Even books written a hundred years ago are out of print and nowhere to be found. Countless accounts exist to verify the Bible's survival. Here are just a few:

Alexander Duff, a young Scottish missionary, was shipwrecked on his way to India. He had 800 choice books among his possessions, all of which were lost. When the survivors were safely on shore, they hoped to salvage some of the wreckage. Thirty-nine books were located, but they were practically pulverized and unreadable. Only one book remained intact. The tide washed it ashore. It was Alexander Duff's Bible.[6]

Read Jeremiah 36 (Page 603). Write a brief summary of the first recorded attempt by evil men to destroy God's Word.

This wicked king's attempt to destroy the recorded words of God failed. Every attempt to exterminate God's Word has been defeated.

In A.D. 303, the Roman emperor Diocletian destroyed every manuscript of the Bible that could be found. Every copy of any portion that could be located was burned. Thousands of families were martyred for having Bibles in their possession. Twenty years after this apparent extinction of the Bible, when Emperor Constantine wanted to put a New Testament in every church, he offered a reward to anyone who could find a Bible to give to him. Within 24 hours, 50 copies were brought to the emperor.

In Turkey, a patient in a hospital was given a Bible that he took home to his village and proudly showed his friends. A teacher of another religion snatched the Bible from him and tore it in pieces, throwing the pieces in the street. A grocer passing by picked up the pieces to use for wrapping paper. Soon, pages of the entire Bible were scattered over the village. Sometime later when a man selling Bibles came to the village, he was amazed to find 100 people eager to buy a complete Bible.[7]

At the 1938 New York World's Fair, a time capsule was buried, which is due to stay sealed until 6938. The capsule included a toothbrush, a can opener, a Mickey Mouse watch, a fountain pen, and a Bible. When asked why the Bible was the only book included, one of the officials in charge replied that the Bible, of all books familiar to them, would most likely survive through the ages.

These incidents are *symbolic* of the survival of the Bible through all kinds of bitter hostility and attempts to destroy it by burning it, cutting it to pieces, or punishing those who possess it. There has never been a time when the Bible has not met opposition of some kind, but in spite of such violent opposition, it still remains with us today.

Does the Bible say anything about the fact that it is indestructible? Summarize the following verses.

Isaiah 40:8 (Page 547)

Psalm 119:89 (Page 470)

Luke 21:33 (Page 804)

It is as impossible to destroy the Word of God as to destroy God Himself! In spite of all attempts to destroy God's Word, there are more Bibles in the world today than ever before.

EVIDENCE OF HARMONY – The books of the Bible, written over a period of 1,500 years by different authors, present a common theme and unusual harmony.

Scholars say that God used 40 men from varied backgrounds to write the text of the Bible. These men had very little in common. Moses, who wrote the first five books of the Old Testament, was a well-educated man, as was Paul, who wrote 13 of the New Testament books. On the other hand, Peter, who wrote two of the New Testament books, was a fisherman.

Other writers of the Bible came from many different walks of life:

Joshua was a military general.

Nehemiah was a king's servant.

David was a shepherd, poet, musician, and king.

Solomon was a king.

Jeremiah was a prophet.

Ezekiel was a priest.

Daniel was a prime minister.

Amos was a herdsman.

Matthew was a tax collector.

Luke was a physician.

John was a fisherman.

These men wrote God's words in many different places: in the wilderness, in a palace, on a hillside, during a military campaign, in times of peace, in times of war, in prison, and while traveling in exile. God used their abilities or He overcame their inabilities and spoke His words through them.

In spite of the fact that the Bible is a library of books written by men from different walks of life over a period of 1,500 years, *it has one primary theme.* These books possess a unity that can only be explained by divine inspiration.

The unifying theme of the Bible is Jesus Christ.

From Moses, who wrote the first book of the Bible, to John, who wrote the last book, the composition of the complete Bible took about 16 centuries. This can be compared to the time period from around 400 A.D. until now. Think how much confusion there is in the writings of 40 authors on any subject covering that span of time! In today's society, two news services sometimes present completely different views of an event that happened that very day. Imagine what could happen with 40 different authors over 1,500 years.

The Bible was written in three different languages on three different continents: Asia, Africa, and Europe. All these factors would seem to make harmony in the Bible impossible. Nevertheless, the Bible has one central theme and one continuous message, presented in perfect harmony.

Following are several subthemes related to the major theme carried throughout the Bible. An Old Testament verse expressing a subtheme is given below. Read the following New Testament verses and write each one below its Old Testament counterpart.

Romans 8:28 (Page 863)   Luke 6:27-28 (Page 786)

John 3:3 (Page 811)   Romans 6:23 (Page 861)

1 John 4:8 (Page 943)

1. The Love of God

   Old Testament – Jeremiah 31:3 (Page 598)

   "Long ago the LORD said to Israel: 'I have loved you, my people, with an everlasting love. With unfailing love I have drawn you to myself.'"

   New Testament Verse _____

2. The Wages of Sin

   Old Testament – Ezekiel 18:20 (Page 638)

   "The person who sins is the one who will die ... wicked people will be punished for their own wickedness."

   New Testament Verse _____

3. New Birth

   Old Testament – Ezekiel 36:26-27 (Page 655)

   "And I will give you a new heart, and I will put a new spirit in you. I will take out your stony, stubborn heart and give you a tender, responsive heart. And I will put my Spirit in you so that you will follow my decrees and be careful to obey my regulations."

   New Testament Verse _____

4. Treatment of Enemies

   Old Testament – Proverbs 25:21 (Page 499)

   "If your enemies are hungry, give them food to eat. If they are thirsty, give them water to drink."

   New Testament Verse _____

5. God's Plans for His People

   Old Testament – Genesis 50:20 (Page 53)

   "You intended to harm me, but God intended it all for good. He brought me to this position so I could save the lives of many people."

   New Testament Verse _____

The unifying theme of the Bible is Jesus Christ. The Old Testament predicts His coming. The books of Moses, the books of the Prophets, and the Psalms are full of prophecies of Him, symbolic representations of Him, and revelations of His mission on the earth. In the New Testament, Jesus Christ is revealed as the Savior. The Gospels (first four books of the New Testament) tell of His birth, life, and death. The book of Acts and the New Testament letters present Him as Priest to His people. The book of Revelation forecasts that He will be King over all people. We will be learning more about Jesus in the next chapter.

EVIDENCE OF AUTHOR COMMITMENT –
The New Testament writers abandoned their prior beliefs, adopted new ones, and did not reverse their faith, even under persecution or death.

The writers of the New Testament truly believed in their message. They backed it up with action and unwavering dedication. Due to these new beliefs, the writers were persecuted and martyred. If they had fabricated the message of the New Testament, wouldn't they have recanted rather than suffer horrible persecution and death? Not one recanted – even though most were martyred for their faith and the apostle John spent years in exile in prison.

Most New Testament writers were eyewitnesses to the events they defended. They witnessed or heard firsthand accounts of Jesus' life, death, and resurrection. They witnessed Jesus performing more than 30 miracles. All the New Testament writers had undeniable proof of Jesus' existence. They were willing to die for their message because they verified it themselves!

THINK IT OVER

How does this differ from those around the world who are "martyrs" in accordance with their beliefs?

Today's martyrs, no matter what their religion, have not been eyewitnesses to the message they proclaim. We know they're sincere – but they don't have firsthand knowledge of the truth.

In New Testament times, the writers had every reason to deny their faith – persecution and even death – but they remained faithful to their message! They would have known, for sure, if what they were dying for was false.

EVIDENCE OF GOD'S POWER – The Bible demonstrates power in the lives of those who obey it.

The reason for that is because the Bible proclaims the power of God.

> **What is God's Word compared to in Hebrews 4:12 (Page 922)?**

This verse says that God's Word is alive, powerful, and penetrating. It reveals the condition of our hearts and communicates God's message to us.

> **What does 2 Timothy 3:16-17 (Page 915) mean?**

We sometimes speak of the work of a gifted writer, poet, or musician as being inspired. But when we say the Bible is "inspired" by God, we mean something entirely different.

It is interesting to note that the Greek word translated inspired (theopneustos) in this verse is used only once in the Bible. It means "breathed out from God."[8] The verse says, "Every Scripture is God-breathed."(NIV)

The Old Testament declares 3,800 times that it expresses words of God: "God said" or according to another translation, "Thus says the Lord."[9]

> **Underline the phrases in the following verses that show God spoke to the writers of the Old Testament in an audible voice.**
>
> **Exodus 34:27 (Page 72) –** *"Then the LORD said to Moses, "Write down all these instructions, for they represent the terms of the covenant I am making with you and with Israel.""*
>
> **Exodus 3:4 (Page 45) –** *"When the LORD saw Moses coming to take a closer look, God called to him from the middle of the bush, 'Moses! Moses!'*

'Here I am!' Moses replied."

Isaiah 6:8 (Page 521) – *"Then I heard the Lord asking, 'Whom should I send as a messenger to this people? Who will go for us?' I said, 'Here I am. Send me.'"*

Jeremiah 1:9 (Page 570) – *"Then the LORD reached out and touched my mouth and said, 'Look, I have put my words in your mouth!'"*

These Old Testament references tell us that God sometimes spoke in an audible voice to the men He used to write the Bible. He told the men to write what He said.

The New Testament authors also declared that the words they wrote came from God. Read the following verses and summarize where their messages originated.

Galatians 1:11-12 (Page 890)

2 Peter 3:15 (Page 939)

1 John 1:5 (Page 941)

Read 2 Peter 3:2 (Page 939). How does this verse validate the Old Testament?

The Jewish people at the time of Christ believed that the Scriptures were divinely inspired. In Acts 1:16 (Page 830), Peter says, "'Brothers ... the Scriptures had to be fulfilled concerning Judas, who guided those who arrested Jesus. This was predicted long ago by the Holy Spirit, speaking through King David.'"

The people accepted the same books we now have in the Old Testament as God-given and authoritative. Acts 3:18, 21 (Page 832) says, "But God was fulfilling what all the prophets had foretold about the Messiah – that he must suffer these things. For he must remain in heaven until the time for the final restoration of all things, as God promised long ago through his holy prophets."

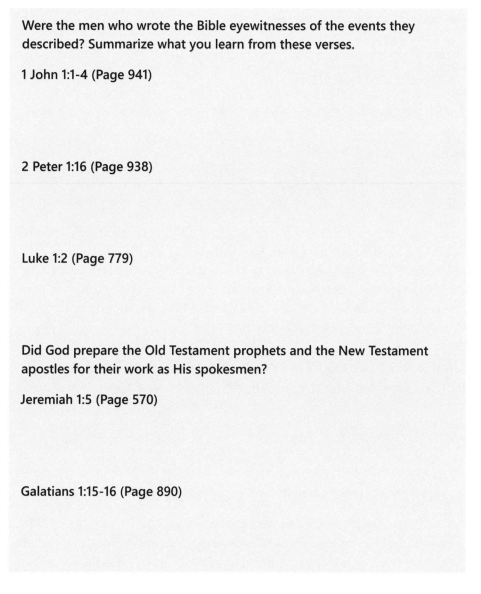

Were the men who wrote the Bible eyewitnesses of the events they described? Summarize what you learn from these verses.

1 John 1:1-4 (Page 941)

2 Peter 1:16 (Page 938)

Luke 1:2 (Page 779)

Did God prepare the Old Testament prophets and the New Testament apostles for their work as His spokesmen?

Jeremiah 1:5 (Page 570)

Galatians 1:15-16 (Page 890)

The men who wrote it did not fully understand the implications of their own teaching, as we are told in 1 Peter 1:12 (Page 934).

In the early years of Christianity, the New Testament books were called the "Christian Scriptures." The early Christians recognized them as coming from the hand of God. During the second century, the "Hebrew

Scriptures" and the "Christian Scriptures" were placed together as books of equal divine inspiration and authority.

The Bible is the infallible revelation of the infallible God, meaning He is not capable of error. But, is the Bible still a source of truth about the meaning of life and about God?

Is the Bible important to us today? Why?

Romans 15:4 (Page 868)

2 Timothy 3:16 (Page 915)

Write your conclusion concerning the inspiration and authority of the Bible.

God's Word will endure forever. He protects His Word through the ages of time and through the necessary translations (since it was originally written in Hebrew, Greek, and Aramaic). We can be confident that God has preserved His Word for us. Whatever the Bible teaches on any subject is authoritative truth revealed by God.

Divine inspiration makes the Bible the Word of God, not just a book that contains the Word of God.

REAL LIFE – BLANCA SOTO

I was lonely. As a young wife and mother living with my in-laws who only spoke Spanish, it was a rough time.

While sitting in my doctor's waiting room one day, I noticed a Bible. I didn't own a Bible, so I opened it. As I sat there reading, the words brought me comfort. So, I grabbed it on my way out and took it with me. I needed to read more!

When I got a job at a hair salon, one of my clients invited me to a Bible study in her home. At that first study, I learned how to look up Bible verses. I sat amazed as others in the group looked up verses – and got something out of what they read!

As I continued to look up verses and study the Bible, my spirit woke up! As a child, I had attended church every Sunday and we said our prayers, so I knew of Jesus, but I didn't know Him until then.

I eventually hosted my own Bible study. Eight friends and clients showed up, none with any experience of studying the Bible. I prayed, loved on them, and guided them gently. And through the years, I've seen Bible reading change many lives.

In Chapter 3, we'll discover some of these evidences for Jesus Christ. Who was He and what proof is there for His existence? Was He just a man or is He God?

CLOSING PRAYER

Dear God, thank You for the power of Your Word. We are thankful to know that we can rely on it and know it is truth. We are glad we can read the very words of the Creator of the universe – the One who holds the universe in His hands. Amen.

FOCUS POINTS

What are the key evidences for the validity of the Bible?

- The Bible stands alone as the best-preserved literary work of all history.
- Archaeology presents compelling evidence that the Bible is accurate in what it describes.
- The Bible has proven to be completely accurate in the prophecies that have been fulfilled.
- Through the years, the Bible has proved to be indestructible.
- The books of the Bible, written over a period of 1,500 years by different authors, present a common theme and unique harmony.
- The New Testament writers abandoned their prior beliefs, adopted new ones, and did not reverse their faith, even under persecution or death.
- The Bible demonstrates power in the lives of those who obey it. The reason? The Bible shares the power of God.

DIG DEEPER – Evidence of the Bible

Josh McDowell and Sean McDowell, *Evidence that Demands a Verdict: Life-Changing Truth for a Skeptic World*, Thomas Nelson, 2017.

Josh McDowell, *God-Breathed: The Undeniable Power and Reliability of Scripture*, Barbour Publishing, 2015.

Randall Price, *The Stones Cry Out: What Archaeology Reveals About the Truth of the Bible*, Harvest House Publishers, 1997.

CHAPTER 3

Who is This Jesus?

As we learned in the last chapter, the major theme of the Bible is Jesus Christ including His message to the world. But, who is this Jesus? Was He a historical figure in the world? Did He really live?

If Jesus really lived on the earth at a point in history, surely there is evidence of His existence in historical records.

EVIDENCE OF JESUS – Historians and other nonbiblical writers serve as proof of Jesus Christ's existence and ministry.

When we study the works of scholars in the world today, we find that they believe Jesus was a historical figure who lived on the earth about 2,000 years ago. They don't deny His many charitable acts.

It is interesting to note that the major world religions recognize Jesus as a historical figure. Muslims see Him as a great prophet, Jewish people see Him as either a false teacher or a rabbi whose teachings have been twisted, some Buddhists see Jesus as an enlightened one, and Hindu tradition also speaks of Jesus. No other religious figure receives acclaim in other religions around the world to the extent that Jesus does.

Historical documents also speak of Jesus. Flavius Josephus (joe-see-fus), the greatest Jewish historian of his time, who in A.D. 66 was commander of Jewish forces in Galilee, wrote the following in the *Antiquities of the Jews*.

"Now, there was about this time Jesus, a wise man, if it be lawful to call Him a man, for He was a doer of wonderful works, a teacher of such men as receive the truth with pleasure. He drew over to Him both many of the Jews, and many of the Gentiles. He was the Christ, and when Pilate, at the suggestion of the principal men among us, had condemned Him to the cross, those that loved Him at the first did not forsake Him; for He appeared to them alive again the third day, as the divine prophets had foretold these and ten thousand other wonderful things concerning Him. And the tribe of Christians, so named from Him are not extinct at this day."[1]

This Jewish historian spoke of Jesus as an actual historical person who walked the earth. While his comments about Jesus' status as "the Christ" are disputed by some, many scholars believe Josephus recognized Jesus as a real person in history.

Cornelius Tacitus was a Roman historian (A.D. 112) who, in writing of the reign of Nero, spoke of Christ being put to death by Pontius Pilate.

Ten non-Christian historians mention Jesus within 150 years of Jesus' life. In comparison, during the same 150 years, there are only nine non-Christian sources who mention Tiberius Caesar, the Roman emperor at the time of Jesus. What if we count the Christian sources? The authors who mention Jesus outnumber those referring to Tiberius 43 to 10![2]

HISTORICAL FACT: By piecing together the 10 non-Christian sources regarding Jesus, we learn many facts about Him:

- Jesus lived during the time of Tiberius Caesar
- He lived a virtuous life
- He was a wonder-worker
- He was acclaimed to be the Messiah
- He was crucified under Pontius Pilate
- He was crucified on the eve of the Jewish Passover
- Darkness and an earthquake occurred when He died
- His disciples believed He rose from the dead
- His disciples were willing to die for their belief
- Christianity spread rapidly as far as Rome
- His disciples denied the Roman gods and worshipped Jesus as God[3]

The sources quoted are just a small sample of the evidence which testifies to the historical reliability of the record of the life of Jesus Christ as reported in the New Testament. History reports that Jesus lived, was worshiped as God, was crucified, buried, and rose again. He changed the course of the world's history so drastically that He literally split history in two. Time is measured before and after His coming. B.C. means "before Christ" and A.D. is the abbreviation for the phrase which means "in the year of the Lord."[4] Nonbelievers, as well as believers, acknowledge Jesus Christ every time they write A.D. in a date – the year of the Lord.

EVIDENCE OF JESUS – Early church leaders support the Bible's view of Jesus Christ.

The Bishop of Antioch, Ignatius (A.D. 70-110), frequently quoted from the Gospels, as well as 13 of the other New Testament books. He was later martyred.

Clement of Alexandria (A.D. 150-212) wrote of Christ, quoting from all but three books of the New Testament. Origen (A.D. 185-253), in his more than 6,000 works, quoted the New Testament more than 18,000 times.

These men wrote about the Lord Jesus as the Christ, the Messiah, the Son of God. What historians wrote agreed with the Scripture writings. The early church leaders wrote in agreement with the New Testament and quoted Scripture to document their writings.

Now we will look at the New Testament – our best and most accurate source of information – and see what the Bible says about Jesus.

EVIDENCE OF JESUS – The Bible presents eyewitness testimony about Jesus.

Biblical authors present details about Jesus that only an eyewitness would know, and they wrote down their accounts within 15 to 40 years after the death of Jesus.

> **Read the following verses and write the words or phrases that indicate the author was writing firsthand knowledge.**
>
> **Acts 3:15 (Page 832)**
>
>
> **2 Peter 1:16 (Page 938)**
>
>
> **1 John 1:1-2 (Page 941)**

These are just a sampling of the eyewitness statements used in the New Testament. Scholars have dissected the books of John, Luke, and half of Acts and have found more than 140 details that have been proven authentic or historically accurate, including more than 30 historical people.[5]

How do we know that the authors didn't take historical facts and embellish them into a fictional story?

> **Listed below are four evidences suggesting the authors didn't make up their accounts about Jesus. Match the evidence with the corresponding verse.**
>
> a. The writers disclosed embarrassing incidents about themselves.
>
> b. The writers researched their facts and presented truth.
>
> c. The writers shared how Jesus was rejected and called names.

d. The writers were persecuted and willing to die for their beliefs.

   _____ 2 Corinthians 11:24-25 (Page 888)

   _____ Luke 1:1-4 (Page 779)

   _____ Mark 14:32-37 (Page 775-776)

   _____ John 10:19-20 (Page 819)
   (Jesus is being spoken about in this passage.)

New Testament authors presented their eyewitness testimony and took care in presenting the facts. They also used facts that their readers could know and verify.

EVIDENCE OF JESUS –
The prophecies of the Old Testament have been fulfilled through Jesus in the New Testament.

A collection of well over 100 prophecies in the Old Testament talk about the future Messiah. Multiple authors spoke of this Messiah over approximately 1,000 years. With the discovery of the Dead Sea Scrolls, we know that these prophecies were written centuries before Jesus arrived on earth as a baby.

In Luke 24:44 (Page 808), Jesus said, "When I was with you before, I told you that everything written about me in the law of Moses and the prophets and in the Psalms must be fulfilled."

Several prophecies of the Old Testament, which are fulfilled and recorded in the New Testament, are given below. Match each New Testament passage with its Old Testament counterpart by writing the correct New Testament verse on the line by the Old Testament reference.

   a. Matthew 2:1 (Page 734)   g. Mark 1:2-4 (Page 761)

   b. Matthew 2:14-15 (Page 734)   h. Mark 14:10 (Page 775)

   c. Matthew 2:16-18 (Page 734)   i. Luke 1:32-33 (Page 779)

   d. Matthew 21:2, 4-5 (Page 751)   j. John 1:11 (Page 809)

   e. Matthew 27:33-36 (Page 759)   k. John 19:33 (Page 827)

   f. Matthew 28:5-6 (Page 760)

Prophecies and Their Fulfillment in Jesus Christ

Heir to the throne of David

Isaiah 9:7 – (700 years B.C.) _____

> *"His government and its peace will never end. He will rule with fairness and justice from the throne of his ancestor David for all eternity. The passionate commitment of the LORD of Heaven's Armies will make this happen!"*

Place of birth

Micah 5:2 – (700 years B.C.) _____

> *"But you, O Bethlehem Ephrathah, are only a small village among all the people of Judah. Yet a ruler of Israel, whose origins are in the distant past, will come from you on my behalf."*

Babies killed

Jeremiah 31:15 – (600 years B.C.) _____

> *"This is what the LORD says: 'A cry is heard in Ramah— deep anguish and bitter weeping. Rachel weeps for her children, refusing to be comforted—for her children are gone.'"*

Flight to Egypt and return from Egypt

Hosea 11:1 – (700 years B.C.) _____

> *"'When Israel was a child, I loved him, and I called my son out of Egypt.'"*

Rejected by His own people

Isaiah 53:3 – (700 years B.C.) _____

> *"He was despised and rejected—a man of sorrows, acquainted with deepest grief. We turned our backs on him and looked the other way. He was despised, and we did not care."*

John the Baptist

Isaiah 40:3 – (700 years B.C.) _____

> *"Listen! It's the voice of someone shouting, 'Clear the way through the wilderness for the LORD! Make a straight highway through the wasteland for our God!'"*

Triumphal Entry

> Zechariah 9:9 – (500 years B.C.) _____

> "... Look, your king is coming to you. He is righteous and victorious, yet he is humble, riding on a donkey—riding on a donkey's colt."

Betrayal by a friend

> Psalm 41:9 – (1000 years B.C.) _____

> "Even my best friend, the one I trusted completely, the one who shared my food, has turned against me."

Soldiers gambled for His coat

> Psalm 22:18 – (1000 years B.C.) _____

> "They divide my garments among themselves and throw dice for my clothing."

No bones broken

> Psalm 34:20 – (1000 years B.C.) _____

> "For the LORD protects the bones of the righteous; not one of them is broken!"

To be resurrected

> Psalm 16:10 – (1000 years B.C.) _____

> "For you will not leave my soul among the dead or allow your holy one to rot in the grave."

What are the odds that one man would fulfill even a handful of these prophecies? A number of scholars have calculated some conservative odds of these events happening to the same man. "If we analyze just a few of the more specific prophecies in the Old Testament, that were later fulfilled in the Person of Jesus Christ, we are stunned by the statistical impossibility of such an historical reality. As an illustration, we have inserted some conservative 'odds' alongside seven established prophecies." (from AllAboutGOD.com)[6]

Messianic Prophecies	What are the Odds Without God?
Jesus would be a descendant of David.	$1:10^4$ (1 in 10,000)
Jesus would be born in Bethlehem.	$1:10^5$ (1 in 100,000)

Messianic Prophecies	What are the Odds Without God?
Jesus would be betrayed by a friend for 30 pieces of silver.	$1:10^6$ (1 in 1,000,000)
Jesus would be crucified.	$1:10^6$ (1 in 1,000,000)
Jesus would first present Himself as King 173,880 days from the decree of Artaxerxes to rebuild Jerusalem.	$1:10^6$ (1 in 1,000,000)
Total Probability	$1:10^{27}$ (1 in 100 billion, billion, billion)

These prophecies are just a sampling of those fulfilled through Jesus Christ, but they make quite a statement!

EVIDENCE OF JESUS – The New Testament presents reliable information concerning Jesus Christ.

The Bible presents Jesus as eternal, present at creation, and active through the Old Testament. As a fulfillment of prophecy, God sent Jesus to be born of a virgin, to minister on earth, and die a cruel death by crucifixion. Jesus was resurrected on the third day, seen by many people, and then He ascended into heaven.

In biblical times, names were very significant since they revealed important characteristics of the person. The greatness and the perfection of Jesus' nature could not be expressed adequately in one name, so Jesus was addressed with many names.

The Bible says God has given Jesus a "name above all other names" (Philippians 2:9). The more we learn about His names, the better we will know Him. Jesus Christ is true to the meaning of each of His names and they are all in harmony with His work and His character.

List the names Jesus is given in each of the following verses:

Matthew 1:21 (Page 733)

What does this name mean?

Matthew 1:23 (Page 733)

What does this name mean?

The Old Testament also gives titles for Jesus. Isaiah 9:6 says, "For a child is born to us, a son is given to us. The government will rest on his shoulders. And he will be called: Wonderful Counselor, Mighty God, Everlasting Father, Prince of Peace."

What did the following people call Jesus?

The Samaritans – John 4:39-42 (Page 812)

Martha – John 11:27 (Page 820)

Thomas – John 20:28 (Page 828)

God – Matthew 17:5 (Page 748)

Jesus reveals to us what God is like. John 14:9 (Page 823) says that whoever has seen Jesus has seen the Father. Hebrews 1:3 (Page 920) (says, "The Son radiates God's own glory and expresses the very character of God ..." Did you notice that? The "very character." Jesus has the very character of God. He possesses all the qualities of deity. In Him, we see God's righteousness, purity, judgment, character, power, and great love.

What did Jesus call Himself?

John 6:35 (Page 814)

John 8:12 (Page 817)

John 10:9 (Page 819)

John 10:11 (Page 819)

John 11:25 (Page 820)

Which one of these names is most meaningful to you in your present life circumstances? Why?

Did you notice that many times when Jesus shared His name, He began with the words, "I Am"? The Jewish people knew God's name to be "I Am," meaning the eternal, self-existent One (Exodus 3:14, Page 45). When Jesus used the phrase "I Am" in reference to Himself, His listeners understood that He was revealing the fact that He is God. This caused the religious leaders much concern.

What did the religious leaders ask Jesus in John 10:23-24 (Page 819)?

What was Jesus' answer in John 10:30 (Page 819)?

How did the people and religious leaders react to Jesus' answer? John 10:31-33 (Page 819)

What did Jesus do that only God can do? Mark 2:1-12 (see verse 5) (Page 762)

At His trial Jesus was asked, "Are you the Messiah, the Son of the Blessed One?" What was His answer? Mark 14:61-62 (Page 776)

Jesus' answer was called blasphemy and He was condemned to death by the religious leaders. Later, the crowd of people condemned Him to death. Their reason is given in John 19:7 (Page 827). Jesus was condemned to death by His own testimony when He told who He really is!

Read the Old Testament verses written out below. Then read the New Testament verse from your Bible. Write the name or title given to both God and Jesus.

Old Testament: *"The LORD is my shepherd; I have all that I need."* – Psalm 23:1

New Testament: John 10:14-15 (Page 819)

Old Testament: *"No longer will you need the sun to shine by day, nor the moon to give its light by night, for the LORD your God will be your everlasting light, and your God will be your glory."* – Isaiah 60:19

New Testament: John 8:12 (Page 817)

Old Testament: *"This is what the LORD says—Israel's King and Redeemer, the LORD of Heaven's Armies: 'I am the First and the Last; there is no other God.'"* – Isaiah 44:6

New Testament: Revelation 1:17-18 (Page 949)

Old Testament: *"So all the world from east to west will know there is no other God. I am the LORD, and there is no other."* – Isaiah 45:6

New Testament: John 13:13 (Page 822)

These and many other Bible references clearly state that Jesus Christ is God. God, in the Person of Jesus Christ, was born in Bethlehem, performed miracles, taught the multitudes, lived a perfect life as a man, allowed Himself to be put to death for the sin of the world, rose from the dead, and ascended bodily into heaven.

Tell in your own words what these verses say about Jesus' nature.

Hebrews 2:17 (Page 921)

Hebrews 7:26 (Page 924)

1 Peter 2:21-22 (Page 935)

Jesus Christ was tempted in every way that we are, but He did not sin. Read Hebrews 4:14-16 (Page 922). Those who knew Jesus best were convinced that He is God. In Matthew 14:33 (Page 746), Jesus disciples worshipped Him and said, "You really are the Son of God."

Jesus is God.[7] He is the very source of life – men could not kill Him. He died because He voluntarily laid down His life. He died on the cross as a sacrifice for our sins. A Roman officer standing in front of the cross saw everything that happened. When he saw Jesus die, he said, "This man was really the Son of God!" (Mark 15:39, Page 777). No one ever talked, lived, or died as Jesus did.

As God, Jesus humbled Himself and became human by being born as a man.

The Bible proves that Jesus was human in every way. But He was "the visible image of the invisible God" (Colossians 1:15, Page 903) at the same time. We cannot separate the two. Because Jesus was both man and God, the things that happened to Him and the things He did seem to be a paradox.

REAL LIFE – LIZ SINGER

I rejected religion at age 17 after a hurtful experience with my church. By my mid-50s and a successful medivac pilot for organ donations, I was surrounding myself with spiritual replacements that made me feel good— meditation, yoga, and speaking to spirits.

One day at the gym, I noticed a lady running on the treadmill. As we both left the gym that day, I initiated a conversation by complimenting her runner's form. What she said completely surprised me, "Do you know Jesus?" I responded, "Not as well as I should." She invited me to church and that simple invite initiated a journey that would change my life. I walked into her beautiful New England church the following Sunday and felt God's love like never before.

A church advertisement for a Bible study called "Why Believe?" caught my eye. Since that was the question I needed answered, I joined! During that Bible study, I learned that Jesus is more than just an historical figure and a moral teacher. He loves me and He died for me. Over time and as I kept studying God's Word, my life changed and I can say, "I believe!"

The following Bible references show Jesus' experiences as both man and God. After each verse, write the word that tells what happened in His manhood or as God.

Matthew 21:18 (Page 751): As man, He was _____ .

John 6:35 (Page 814): As God, He is the _____ .

John 4:7 (Page 811): As man, He was _____ .

John 7:38 (Page 816): As God, He is the _____ (He satisfies our thirst).

John 4:6 (Page 811): As man, He was _____ .

Matthew 11:28 (Page 742): As God, He gives _____ .

Hebrews 2:10 (Page 921): As man, He _____ .

Matthew 4:23 (Page 735): As God, He _____ .

Matthew 4:1 (Page 735): As man, He was _____ .

James 1:13 (Page 930): As God, He cannot be _____ .

John 11:35 (Page 820): As man, He _____ at a grave.

John 11:43-44 (Page 820): As God, He called the dead to _____ .

Mark 15:37 (Page 777): As man, He _____ .

Revelation 1:18 (Page 949): As God, He is _____ .

The greatest proof that Jesus Christ is divine is His resurrection from the dead.

EVIDENCE OF JESUS – The Resurrection of Jesus Christ has significant proofs.

The teaching that Jesus rose from the dead is the event upon which the Christian faith is based. Paul said, "... And if Christ has not been raised, then all our preaching is useless, and your faith is useless." (1 Corinthians 15:14, Page 879).

Read about Jesus' resurrection in Matthew 28:1-9 (Page 760).

The resurrection of Jesus is a necessary condition of the Christian faith. Read Romans 10:9 (Page 864). Without the resurrection, we would have no one to put our faith in for forgiveness of sin.

What are the facts of the resurrection? Was the tomb actually empty? Was foul play involved? Did anyone see Jesus following His resurrection?

One of the facts of Jesus' life that is undisputed is the fact that His tomb was found empty. In Matthew 28:11-15 (Page 760), read how the Jewish authorities reacted to the disciples' claim that the tomb was empty. They bribed the soldiers! Instead of disproving the disciples' claims, they devised a plan to cover it up. They fabricated a lie for the soldiers to report.

THINK ABOUT IT: Could the soldiers have been asleep? If the soldiers were asleep, how would they have known what happened to Jesus' body? Why would they admit to sleeping on the job when the punishment would have been severe, possibly death?

The biblical authors say that Christ appeared to more than 500 different people after He rose from the dead. There are as many as 12 different appearances of Christ. Could these people have been experiencing hallucinations? The variety of situations and the number of people involved makes group hallucination impossible. These eyewitnesses were also alive, and easy to find, when the Gospels were written, making it difficult to invent stories.

Jesus was physically seen and touched by numerous people after He rose from the dead. Read John 20:24-28 (Page 828).

After Jesus' resurrection, we see a transformation in His disciples. At the time of the crucifixion, these men were scared, confused, and scattered. Something significant would have to occur to pull these men together again, giving them courage and the conviction to die for their beliefs. They went from hiding in secret to having the boldness to die for the risen Christ. The men with the most direct knowledge of what really happened to Jesus were the most fervent in insisting He was resurrected!

Read how their demeanor and purpose changed after the resurrection in Acts 4:13 (Page 833). As they proclaimed the message of the resurrected Christ, the church grew quickly.

So where is Jesus now? Read Hebrews 12:2 (Page 927).

Jesus Christ is a real, historical Person. Not only was He a real, physical Person, He still is a real, living Person. He makes Christianity different from all religions, for He is the center of Christianity. Jesus Christ lived about 2,000 years ago and is still alive today! He is eternal.

THINK IT OVER

Why does Jesus matter? How does He affect me?

Jesus claimed to be God and He proved it! He fulfilled the prophecies written in the Old Testament hundreds of years in advance. He lived a sinless life. He performed numerous miracles. He prophesied His death and resurrection and then He accomplished them! Jesus is God!

Jesus lived on this earth in a human body, lived a life in complete harmony with God, lived in complete obedience to God's will, and died a physical death. He arose from the grave. He is alive today. He is personally and intimately involved in the lives of those who have received Him into their lives.

There are other religions that accept the fact that Jesus lived and died. What makes Christianity different? Jesus' entrance into the life of a person changes that person. For the first time, that person is really alive. Before he received Christ, he was spiritually dead in his sins. After receiving Christ – the source of life – he becomes alive! Christians are people who are complete because they have Christ in their lives. We will learn more about that in our next chapter.

PRAYER BY GUIDE

Dear God, Thank You for sending Your Son, Jesus, to die on the cross for our sin and be raised to life again. Thank You for providing a way for us to have eternal life with You. In Jesus' name, Amen.

FOCUS POINTS

- Historians and other nonbiblical writers serve as proof of Jesus Christ's existence and ministry.
- Early church leaders support the Bible's view of Jesus Christ.
- The Bible presents eyewitness testimony about Jesus.
- The prophecies of the Old Testament have been fulfilled through Jesus in the New Testament.
- The New Testament presents reliable information concerning Jesus Christ.
- The resurrection of Jesus has significant proofs.

DIG DEEPER – Evidence of Jesus

www.AllAboutJesusChrist.org — Articles that answer the question: Who is Jesus?

Ravi Zacharias, *Jesus Among Secular Gods: The Countercultural Claims of Christ*, 2017.

Lee Strobel, *The Case for Christ*, Zondervan, 2016.

Josh McDowell and Sean McDowell, *More than a Carpenter*, Tyndale House Publishers, 2009.

Norman Geisler and Patrick Zukeran, *The Apologetics of Jesus*, Baker Books, 2008.

CHAPTER 4

Why Christianity?

Restaurants encourage us to order our food prepared exactly the way we enjoy it. Coffee shops offer numerous flavors. At this time in history, choice is king! So, what about selecting a religion that is perfect for you? Can we select a religion just like we select a flavor of ice cream? Do all religions ultimately lead to heaven?

To understand the question, "Are all religions equally good?" we need to first define religion.

> **Write your definition of the word "religion." What words come to mind when you think of religion?**

The word "religion" comes from a Latin word which means "to bind, to obligate or to bind by fear." The word portrays the idea of working to gain favor with God or binding oneself to a set of rules. All religions give their followers rites to follow, observances to keep, and ways to perform for the purpose of gaining God's favor. Religion is a man-made way of trying to get right with God.

> **Write your definition of the word "Christian." What words come to mind when you think of a Christian?**

Christianity is a relationship – a relationship between an individual and Jesus Christ.

Study the following evidence that makes Christianity the right choice:

EVIDENCE OF CHRISTIANITY –
Christianity is not only a religion. It is a relationship.

Real Christianity is more than a religion. It is not a denomination, nor a church building. It is not about elaborate traditions or rules. Christianity is a relationship between a person and Jesus Christ.

As we learned in Chapter 1, some religions of the world are atheistic (no god), some are polytheistic (many gods), and some believe in only one God (monotheistic). Most religions of the earth were devised by human beings. Usually a person appeared on the scene and presented himself (or herself) as a religious leader. In some cases, a group acclaimed the person as a leader. Each of these leaders was born, lived, and died as any other person. They searched for truth, but few claimed to have found it.

Jesus stands in extreme contrast to other religious leaders. He not only claimed to know truth, but He stated He is truth. Jesus said, ". . . I am the way, the truth, and the life. No one can come to the Father except through me" (John 14:6, Page 823). He is the truth about God. He is the truth about what God intended man to be. Jesus Christ is the very essence of truth.

Christianity is not based merely on Jesus' teachings, but on Jesus Christ Himself. In other belief systems, it is possible to be part of a religion and not know the founder. Not so with Christianity. A personal relationship with Jesus Christ is the essence of the Christian faith.

REAL LIFE – TINA RIGONI

I had the perfect life with a great husband and three beautiful children. It was just as I had always planned, and I wouldn't have changed a thing. We went to church occasionally and I even taught Sunday School, but it was nothing more than "church" to me. I only talked to God when I needed something. I knew about God's love and His message of hope to us. I understood that I was a sinner and that sin prevents us from knowing joy in the Lord. I knew I was separated from God, but it didn't concern me much. Life was going so well. I didn't need God in my life.

One summer day, my life changed forever when my youngest child, who was three years old, was diagnosed with a strain of E. coli. This toxic bacteria sent my little girl to the hospital and she was in serious condition. I was filled with uncertainty. Why me? What had I done to deserve this? "God, can you even hear me? Are you there?" I felt alone – hopeless – helpless.

There was no cure for my daughter and the doctors had no encouragement. I felt like my ship was sinking, until it eventually hit bottom. My precious little girl died following 33 days of unsuccessful treatment. My whole life stopped. I felt numb.

Had I failed as a parent? I wanted her to be with me, not with Jesus. I didn't know anyone could hurt so much and still keep on living.

A kind neighbor, who was trying to get me out of the house, asked me to go to a Stonecroft lunch with her. I remember the speaker talking about inviting Jesus into my life. I wanted to do everything I could to make sure I would spend eternity in heaven with Jesus and my little girl. I prayed to God that day and asked Him to forgive my sins. I learned that Jesus took the punishment for my sins and I asked Jesus to be my Savior. Jesus came into my life in a real and wonderful way.

God knew my pain. He knew my heart. I depended on Him because I truly knew that He was the only One who could help me through this loss. In His Word, He promises that nothing – not even the greatest tragedy – can separate us from His love. He gives us peace, hope, and even joy in the midst of devastating circumstances.

Before I accepted Jesus, I didn't think I needed Him in my life. I had no personal relationship with Him. I looked good on the outside, but on the inside, I was full of holes. When I accepted Christ, my whole life and outlook changed. My life now is full of peace and joy – and that is no easy task following the death of a child.

I truly came to know Christ through the death of my daughter. Jesus was not only my lighthouse through the storm, but my life preserver.

Tina found religion to be shallow, but a genuine relationship with Jesus brought her peace and joy.

EVIDENCE OF CHRISTIANITY –
Christianity teaches a unique view of salvation.

All religions are not the same. Even those religions which recognize the living God hold conflicting views of what He is like and what He requires of people. It is only logical to recognize that, if God exists, He has the right to say who He is and what He requires of mankind.

The following Bible verses show what God says. Let's study how Christianity differs from the religions of all time. It stands unique among them all. Read the following verses and fill in the blank.

Many world religions accept matter as eternal because their gods did not bring it into being. Christianity believes that the world was created by _____ from nothing (Psalm 33:9, Page 427).

Christianity is centered on the historical event of _____ (1 Corinthians 15:2-7, Page 879).

Christianity is based on the birth, death, and resurrection of Jesus Christ. Christianity states that Jesus lives in all who have received Him and that He is coming to earth again.

Jesus Christ alone has conquered death. The founders and original leaders of all the worldwide religions have died. Their graves can be visited. Their closest followers testified to these deaths. As we learned in the last chapter, Jesus' tomb is empty. The bodily resurrection of Christ is one of the best attested facts of history.

A unique aspect of Christianity is that Christ lives in _____ (Galatians 2:20, Page 891; and Colossians 1:27, Page 903)

Christianity is Christ living in a person. It is not following a set of rules, performing rituals, acting a certain way, or joining a church. A Christian is one who has received the free gift of salvation (deliverance from sin and its consequences). While a typical religion is something you put on – acting and living a certain way – Christianity is an inner reality. It is an inside change which results in a changed behavior. No one deserves it; no one has earned it. God gives right standing with Himself as a free gift.

Most world religions don't teach about sin (anything displeasing to God). Biblical Christianity teaches that _____ (Romans 3:23, Page 859).

The Bible says that human nature cannot _____ (Romans 8:8, Page 862).

Religions of the world say that as humans, we are not tainted by sin. God says that we are _____ (Romans 8:7, Page 862).

The Bible says that _____ as a result of sin (Romans 6:23, Page 861).

Sin separates us from a God who is holy. Until our sin is taken care of, we cannot have a relationship with God.

The religions of the world teach that salvation or enlightenment (an eternal state of goodness and understanding) are based on the things their followers are told to do. Each religion establishes a set of religious rites, commands, restrictions, and principles to follow.

> Unlike other systems of faith, Christianity is not based on
> _____ (Ephesians 2:8-9, Page 896).
>
> Biblical Christianity says that God saved us because
> _____ (2 Timothy 1:9, Page 914).

Religions teach what I must do to reach God. Christianity teaches what God did to reach out to me.

The standard of Christianity is the holiness and perfection of God Himself. Only God would set a standard so high that we could not reach it by ourselves. Due to our sin, we could never be good enough or do enough good deeds. Only Jesus Christ lived a life of perfect holiness and full obedience to God, which proved that He is God.

THINK IT OVER

Some people argue that all religions are based on following and worshiping the same God. They say we may call Him different names and approach Him in different ways, but we are all His children. What do you think? How did you arrive at that conclusion?

God alone has the right to say who He is and what He requires of us. He tells us the answer to that argument in Acts 4:12 (Page 833).

Jesus did not say He would teach people a new way to live or a new system of religion. Instead Jesus said, "I am the way, the truth, and the life" (John 14:6, Page 823). Notice Jesus said "I am the way" – not that I know the way, or that I will teach the way, but that I am the way.

No other religious leader can impart life. What did Jesus say in John 10:10 (Page 819)?

Jesus died to pay the penalty of sin. In this way, He offers full pardon to all who come to Him for forgiveness. He rose from the dead so that He could give His own nature (his character, attitude, love, etc.) to anyone who receives Him by faith.

REAL LIFE – BARBARA CARR

Fear controlled my whole being. I was afraid to be alone day or night. I expected my husband to be my security, but even he came up short of my expectations. I was searching for something to fill the void in my soul – but what was I searching for?

I was active in my church, but I still felt that something was missing. The gap in my spirit remained. One day, a woman invited me to Bible study. This interested me, even though I knew very little about the Bible. I wanted to find out what truth really was. Would I find it in the Bible? I attended the study and felt like the Bible was so connected to my life and what I was going through. Somehow, I knew that my answer was going to be found in the Bible.

I had so many questions. I believed in God, but I also believed if I did enough good things, then good things would happen to me and I would go to heaven. I became active in another church group, thinking that I might find the answers to my questions. This group was made up of people who wanted to help other people know Jesus. I didn't even know Him! How was I going to help other people find Him?

During the meetings, I started to understand. I wasn't going to find my answers in religion or get to heaven by being good or doing good things. Salvation is not something earned or deserved. I learned that I am a sinner and God has requirements – I had come up short. But, because God is forgiving, He made a provision for me. The Bible says that the wages of sin is death, but the gift of God is eternal life. I learned that Jesus, God's Son, came down from heaven as a baby. He grew up with one purpose – to die for all the sin of the world.

Then I learned the clincher: Jesus is God! When Jesus died for sin, He paid the price that I should have paid for my sins. My sins are paid for and Jesus made it possible for me to live in heaven with God forever! The Bible says that God loved the world so much that He gave His only Son, so that everyone who believes in Him may not die but can have eternal life. Jesus offers us life.

It seemed almost too simple. Jesus has already done everything. What did I have to do? I realized there was nothing I could do to earn my way to heaven. I made a conscious decision to believe in Jesus, to accept Him as Savior.

My attitudes began to change, and my Bible study started to make more sense. I started applying what I was learning to everyday activities. I decided to put my trust in Jesus, my Savior.

EVIDENCE OF CHRISTIANITY –
Christianity uses both mind and heart.

God created us with the ability to think, to learn, to reason, and to discern truth. But still some people ask: "Is it a reasonable, logical, and intelligent action to put my faith in the Lord Jesus Christ?"

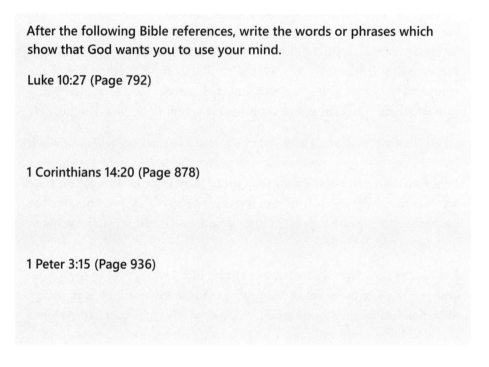

After the following Bible references, write the words or phrases which show that God wants you to use your mind.

Luke 10:27 (Page 792)

1 Corinthians 14:20 (Page 878)

1 Peter 3:15 (Page 936)

When we want to investigate something, we do research, honestly consider our findings, and make our own conclusion. That is what we have done in this Bible study. We have honestly examined the basic evidence concerning the topic of each chapter. We have had an opportunity to think about these things and make our own decisions.

God gave us the ability to think, learn, and reason. He wants us to be reasonable and honest in our thinking. He gives more understanding and wisdom when we need it. If we lack wisdom, He tells us to ask for it. Read James 1:5 (Page 930).

We have investigated the scientific proof of God's existence, the historical and archaeological evidence of the Bible, and the evidence of Jesus being the Son of God. We learned that Jesus was a real, physical Person and that He is still living. These facts make Christianity different from all religions!

Using the knowledge you gained in this study, how would you answer this question: "Who is a Christian?" 1 John 5:11-12 (Page 943).

The following references tell what the Bible says about how to become a Christian. Write a brief summary of each reference.

God's part – Titus 3:4-7 (Page 918)

Our response – John 3:36 (Page 811); Romans 10:9-10 (Page 864)

More is necessary than knowledge about God and the Bible. To know about God's Son, Jesus, is not enough to make a person a Christian. Accepting these ideas requires trust – which the Bible calls faith!

Remember the Real Life story from our first chapter ? Randall Niles was a hard skeptic who was sorting through the evidences of God's existence.

Randall's journey led him down similar topics as we have studied in this course. How did he end up? Let's listen in:

REAL LIFE – RANDALL NILES, CONTINUED (FROM CHAPTER 1)

Although the Christian faith is not based purely on evidence, it is definitely supported by evidence. Faith is not about turning off the brain and merely relying on the heart, or squashing reason in favor of emotion. No, Christian faith is about seeking and knowing Jesus with all facets of the human character. It's not a "blind faith" as I once thought. It's a "calculated faith" based on a preponderance of the evidence. Well, I've collected the evidence, and I've put it on trial. After a number of months in the jury room, I have returned with my personal verdict. Jesus Christ is who He claims to be – the Son of God who came to this earth about 2,000 years ago to offer true and lasting hope for mankind. OK, now what? I intellectually believe, by a preponderance of the evidence, that God exists, that the Bible is true, and that Jesus is His Son. How does this affect me? What is faith, as far as it concerns me?

I love the metaphor of a chair. Find the chair closest to you. Look at it closely. Examine its design. Is it structurally sound? Is it sufficiently engineered? Will the materials chosen by the manufacturer support your weight?

Most likely, you picked a chair that you believe will support you. That's belief. You applied logic, knowledge, and experience to make an informed intellectual decision.

Now sit in the chair. That's faith! At one point, intellectual assent only goes so far. True living requires that we put our beliefs into action. Intellectual belief without actionable faith is hollow and meaningless.[1]

MAKE IT PERSONAL

1. Do you believe God exists?

   O Yes   O No

   If you answered yes, what are you going to do about it?

2. Do you believe the Bible is true?

   O Yes   O No

   If you anvswered yes, what does that mean for you?

3. What do you believe about Jesus?

   O Jesus is only a historical figure.   O Jesus is God.

   If Jesus is God, how will this reality change your life?

It is not enough to know the facts about Jesus Christ. More than our minds and our emotions are involved. We must respond to God's love by believing and receiving Jesus' death on the cross as full payment for our personal sin. Any person who accepts Jesus Christ as Savior receives eternal life in heaven.

If you believe what the Bible says about Jesus, what should you do about it? Read Romans 10:9-13 (Page 864) to find out.

When we personally believe that Jesus died for our sins, we repent of our sins and ask God's forgiveness. We can thank Him for dying in our place and ask Him to live His life in us. By His Holy Spirit, He enters our lives and makes us His children. Through Jesus' death and resurrection, God's justice has been satisfied and we have right standing with God. We are free from guilt.

> If you would like to further explore the roles God's love and mercy play in freedom from sin, read God's Pursuing Love (Page 69) and talk with your Guide.

If you have not received Jesus Christ as your personal Savior and you would like to do so, pray a prayer similar to this. **Saying this prayer or any other prayer will not give you freedom from sin. It is only trusting in Jesus Christ that can provide forgiveness of sins.** This prayer is simply a way to express to God your faith in Him and to thank Him for providing for your forgiveness.

Dear God, I want to be Your child. I confess to You the fact that I have sinned against You. Forgive me. Thank You for sending Jesus to die on the cross for my sin and rise again to give me life. I want Jesus to come into my life and I now receive Him as my Savior and Lord. I believe Your Word and thank You for coming into my life as You said You would. Thank You for giving me eternal life and making me Your child. In Jesus' name, Amen.

Signature _____ Date _____

The Bible says that Christians are those who are sorry for their sins, turn from them, and trust in Jesus Christ. They are created anew in the innermost part of their being by the Holy Spirit.

First Corinthians 6:17 (Page 873) says that Christians are united to Christ. The inner nature of the believer is changed so that his innermost desire turns from disobeying God and serving self to denying self and obeying God.

All who put their trust in Christ are born again into God's family. We have a new life of fellowship with Christ. We have assurance of salvation and a hope beyond this life.

In this study, we have discovered evidence that God exists, that He left a message for us, and that He wants to have a personal relationship with us. We've learned that we have evidence behind our faith. In fact, we can step out in faith knowing that our feet will land on a firm foundation.

CLOSING PRAYER

Dear God, thank You for what we have learned in this study and for the friendships we have made. Help us to take the evidence we have learned and share it with others. Increase our faith and help us to trust You and Your Word. We love You. In Jesus' name, amen.

FOCUS POINTS

What are the key evidences for Christianity?

- Christianity is not a religion. It is a relationship.
- Christianity teaches a unique view of salvation.
- Christianity uses both the mind and the heart.

If you put your trust in God, we have a short Bible study to help you start your new life in Christ. Go to stonecroft.org/know-god and complete the form.

TIME FOR ACTION

One of the keys when studying the Bible is to apply the principles we learn and let God impact our lives in significant and life-changing ways. One of the ways to instigate this is to share what we learn with others. Consider these action-oriented suggestions:

- Review the focus points of each Chapter and share several evidences with a friend or family member.
- Take a walk through nature with a child and talk about the amazing details of creation. Explain that God created it all.
- Select a chapter in the Bible and write a summary paragraph explaining how that chapter is applicable to the world today. Share your observations with a friend.

- Conduct a survey at a local coffee shop or meeting place. Ask several people, "Who is Jesus Christ?" Listen to their answers. If the opportunity arises, tell them what you have learned about who Jesus is.

- Write your own Real Life story and practice presenting it to someone else.

DIG DEEPER – Evidence for Christianity

Max Anders, *New Christian's Handbook*, Thomas Nelson, 2011.

William Lane Craig, *A Reasonable Response: Answers to Tough Questions on God, Christianity, and the Bible*, Moody Publishers, 2013.

Max Lucado, *No Wonder They Call Him the Savior*, Thomas Nelson, 2011.

Ravi Zacharias, *Answering the Biggest Objections to Christianity*, Ravi Zacharias International Ministries, 2015.

Chip Ingram, *Why I Believe: Straight Answers to Honest Questions about God, the Bible, and Christianity*, Baker Books, 2018.

GOD'S PURSUING LOVE

God, who created the universe, is full of love and mercy. He desires for you to personally receive these gifts from Him.

It doesn't matter what has happened in your past. No matter what you've done, no matter what's been done to you, no matter what you regret about how you've lived your life, God's mercy is greater. God understands you – your hopes, your dreams, your frustrations, your loneliness, your heartaches. His love caused Him to pursue us, to leave heaven and come to earth.

"For God so loved the world that he gave his one and only Son, that whoever believes in him shall not perish but have eternal life. For God did not send his Son into the world to condemn the world, but to save the world through him."

– John 3:16-17, NIV

God is love. He is a God of relationship.

God created us to have a real and personal relationship with Him. Sin keeps us from having a loving relationship with God. We all have sinned and been separated from God. We all carry sin's consequences in our lives.

But God the Father loves so deeply that He made a way to close the gap of separation. He sent His Son, Jesus, to earth to live a perfect life with no sin and then to die in our place. Jesus Christ took the punishment for our sin. Jesus is God and He did the work for us.

Nothing we can do will earn us God's love. No good works. No good deeds. No avoidance of evil. "For God made Christ, who never sinned, to be the offering for our sin, so that we could be made right with God through Christ" (2 Corinthians 5:21).

"But God is so rich in mercy, and he loved us so much, that even though we were dead because of our sins, he gave us life when he raised Christ from the dead. (It is only by God's grace that you have been saved!)"

– Ephesians 2:4-5

Jesus Christ paid the penalty for sin when He died on the cross. But He did not stay dead! He came back to life, He rose from the dead. And He is ready to share His life with you.

Jesus is alive today. He offers reconciliation to us. He can give you a new beginning and a newly created life. "This means that anyone who belongs to Christ has become a new person. The old life is gone; a new life has begun!" (2 Corinthians 5:17).

How do you begin this new life? Place your trust in Jesus Christ. Believe that He is God and receive His love. Agree with God about your sin and believe that Jesus came to close the separation between you and God. Ask Jesus to lead your life.

When you trust Jesus Christ, He will live in your life. God's Spirit will live inside you. This Holy Spirit will help you live a life that honors Him.

Do you want to begin this new life? The following prayer is a simple way to express to God your faith in Him and to thank Him for providing for your forgiveness from sin.

You can start today with a few simple words like, "Dear Jesus, I believe that You are God and that You love me and came to save me through Your death and resurrection."

It is only our trust in Jesus Christ that reconciles us to God. Saying this prayer or any other prayer will not give you freedom from sin, they simply communicate our faith to Jesus.

Or you might pray something like this:

> *Jesus, I believe You are the Son of God and that You died on the cross to pay the penalty for my sin. Forgive me. I choose to turn away from my sin and live a life that honors You. I want to follow You and make You the leader of my life. Thank You for Your gift of eternal life and for the Holy Spirit who now has come to live in me. Amen.*

Stonecroft wants to offer you a free publication called A New Beginning. This short Bible study will help you get started on your new faith journey. You can order a free copy by filling out the form found on the lower part of this webpage: stonecroft.org/know-god. The form includes a small box to check to request a downloadable copy of A New Beginning. You will want a Bible. We recommend the New Living Translation (NLT).

May God move mightily in response to your prayers!

ACKNOWLEDGMENTS

We are grateful to the team of people God put together to make this revision of *Why Believe?* possible. We are especially grateful to author MeLissa Houdmann, who used her diligent research and expertise to explain the evidence of the Christian faith.

We also want to thank the Stonecroft family of prayer warriors and funding partners who supported this effort throughout the process. This book took the work of many people, such as the editors, designer, project managers, proofreaders, department leaders, and the list goes on.

We especially thank our independent reviewers who provided excellent guidance. Our goal was to provide a valuable resource to lead people from skeptic to believer. With their help and expertise, we are confident we have reached that goal.

Jeff Laird carefully checked every detail of this study for scientific and apologetic accuracy. Jeff is an Associate Editor, specializing in apologetics, for Got Questions Ministries and is the Managing Editor of BibleRef.com.

C.J. Moore provided the theological review for this work. His close inspection asked necessary questions for clarity of the message. C.J. is a Ph.D. student in Missiology and a Fellow at Midwestern Baptist Theological Seminary in Kansas City, Missouri.

Special thanks to those who use *Why Believe?* to build relationships with seekers, praying for them and guiding them into truth.

To God be the glory forever and ever.

– Stonecroft

FOR GUIDES:
Tips to Lead This Study

Thank you for guiding *Why Believe?*

The purpose of this study is to help people understand the truth of the Christian faith by looking at the evidence for God, the Bible, and Jesus. It's best if your group avoids distractions and disruptions stemming from discussions about doctrinal, social, or political topics on which people disagree.

To help you specifically guide *Why Believe?* we offer these tips:

· Aim for each meeting to last 60 to 90 minutes. These chapters are a little longer than those of other Stonecroft Bible Studies. If time is limited, feel free to divide the lessons in half and take more weeks to complete. Or, you can assign some work in the next chapter to be done before the meeting. Discussion is generated by shared answers to the questions and by reading the Bible verses together.

· Scripture references in *Why Believe?* are accompanied by page numbers found in the *Abundant Life Bible New Living Translation*. This simplifies looking up Scripture verses for those who are unfamiliar with the Bible.

· An answer key is found on Page 76 for many of the questions in the chapters including fill-in-the-blank, matching, and other types of questions. We recommend that before going over the chapter with your participants, you transfer these answers into your copy of the book, as well as find the answers to the remaining questions.

· The proclamation of the Gospel is a high priority for Stonecroft. The Gospel in *Why Believe?* is presented through a Real Life Story, in Lesson 4, and in God's Pursuing Love, a presentation in the back of the book. While doing the lesson, offer the opportunity to go through God's Pursuing Love if a participant desires more information before committing to a relationship with Jesus. God's Pursuing Love is best done with the guide and participant together. The participant reads Scripture and the guide reads the narrative.

· Close to the end of this study, start thinking about next steps. No matter what group participants decide concerning their relationship with Christ, invite them to do another study. We recommend going through *Who is Jesus?*, *What is God Like?*, and *Who is the Holy Spirit?* next. Following these introductory studies, consider the Genesis series, *Growing in the Christian Life* (James) or *Living in God's Will* (Ruth). They can all be found in our store at stonecroft.org/store.

ANSWER KEY

Chapter 2

Page 27

Read the following New Testament verses and write each one below its Old Testament counterpart.

1. The Love of God

   Old Testament – Jeremiah 31:3

   New Testament – <u>1 John 4:8</u>

2. The Wages of Sin

   Old Testament – Ezekiel 18:20

   New Testament – <u>Romans 6:23</u>

3. New Birth

   Old Testament – Ezekiel 36:26-27

   New Testament – <u>John 3:3</u>

4. Treatment of Enemies

   Old Testament – Proverbs 25:21

   New Testament – <u>Luke 6:27-28</u>

5. God's Plans for His People

   Old Testament – Genesis 50:20

   New Testament – <u>Romans 8:28</u>

Page 29

Underline the phrases in the following verses that show God spoke to the writers of the Old Testament in an audible voice.

Exodus 34:27: "Then the LORD <u>said</u> to Moses, 'Write down all these instructions, for they represent the terms of the covenant I am making with you and with Israel.'"

Exodus 3:4: "When the LORD saw Moses coming to take a closer look, God <u>called</u> to him from the middle of the bush, 'Moses! Moses!' 'Here I am!' Moses replied."

Isaiah 6:8: "Then I <u>heard</u> the Lord <u>asking</u>, 'Whom should I send as a messenger to this people? Who will go for us?' I said, 'Here I am. Send me.'"

Jeremiah 1:9: "Then the LORD reached out and touched my mouth and <u>said</u>, 'Look, I have put my words in your mouth!'"

Chapter 3

Page 40

Match the evidence with the corresponding verse.

_d_   2 Corinthians 11:24-25

_b_   Luke 1:1-4

_a_   Mark 14:32-37

_c_   John 10:19-20

Page 42

Prophecies and their Fulfillment in Jesus

Heir to the throne of David

     Isaiah 9:7 – i. Luke 1:32-33

Place of birth

     Micah 5:2 – a. Matthew 2:1

Babies killed

     Jeremiah 31:15 – c. Matthew 2:16-18

Flight to Egypt and return from Egypt

     Hosea 11:1 – b. Matthew 2:14-15

Rejected by His own people

     Isaiah 53:3 – j. John 1:11

John the Baptist

     Isaiah 40:3 – g. Mark 1:2-4

Triumphal Entry

     Zechariah 9:9 – d. Matthew 21:2, 4-5

Betrayal by a friend

     Psalm 41:9 – h. Mark 14:10

Soldiers gambled for His coat

     Psalm 22:18 – e. Matthew 27:33-36

No bones broken

     Psalm 34:20 – k. John 19:33

To be resurrected

     Psalm 16:10 – f. Matthew 28:5-6

Page 44

List the names Jesus is given in each of the following verses:

Matthew 1:21 Jesus

What does this name mean? He will save His people from their sins.

Matthew 1:23 Immanuel

What does this name mean? God is with us.

Page 45

What did the following people call Jesus?

The Samaritans – John 4:39-42 the Savior of the world

Martha – John 11:27 the Messiah, the Son of God

Thomas – John 20:28 my Lord and my God

God – Matthew 17:5 my dearly loved Son

What did Jesus call Himself?

John 6:35 I am the Bread of Life

John 8:12 I am the Light of the World

John 10:9 I am the Gate

John 10:11 I am the Good Shepherd

John 11:25 I am the Resurrection and the Life

Page 46

What did the religious leaders ask Jesus in John 10:23-24? They asked if He was the Messiah.

What was Jesus' answer in John 10:30? "The Father and I are one."

How did the people and religious leaders react to Jesus' answer? They wanted to stone Jesus.

What did Jesus do that only God can do? Forgive sin

What was His answer? "I am"

Page 47

Write the name or title given to both God and Jesus.

New Testament: John 10:14-15 Shepherd

New Testament: John 8:12 Light

New Testament: Revelation 1:17-18 First and Last

New Testament: John 13:13 Lord

After each verse, write the word that tells what happened in His manhood or as God.

Matthew 21:18: As man, He was hungry .

John 6:35: As God, He is the Bread of Life .

John 4:7: As man, He was thirsty .

John 7:38: As God, He is the living water .

John 4:6: As man, He was tired .

Matthew 11:28: As God, He gives rest to the weary .

Hebrews 2:10: As man, He suffered .

Matthew 4:23: As God, He healed every kind of disease and illness .

Matthew 4:1: As man, He was tempted .

James 1:13: As God, He cannot be tempted .

John 11:35: As man, He wept at a grave.

John 11:43-44: As God, He called the dead to rise .

Mark 15:37: As man, He died .

Revelation 1:18: As God, He is alive forever .

Chapter 4

Christianity believes that the world was created by God from nothing. Psalm 33:9

Christianity is centered on the historical event of Jesus' death and resurrection . 1 Corinthians 15:2-7

A unique aspect of Christianity is that Christ lives in believers . Galatians 2:20; Colossians 1:27

Biblical Christianity teaches that everyone has sinned and falls short . Romans 3:23

The Bible says that human nature cannot please God . Romans 8:8

Religions of the world say that as humans, we are not tainted by sin. God says that we are hostile to God . Romans 8:7

The Bible says that we will die as a result of sin. Romans 6:23

Unlike other systems of faith, Christianity is not based on good things we have done . Ephesians 2:8-9

Biblical Christianity says that God saved us because that was his plan, to show us his grace through Christ Jesus . 2 Timothy 1:9

ENDNOTES

Chapter 1

1 *What Happened to Me: Reflections of a Journey* by Randall Niles, iUniverse, ©2004. Excerpts from www.allaboutthejourney.org/my-worldview.html, www.allaboutthejourney.org/realism-and-naturalism.html, and www.allaboutthejourney.org/critical_thinking-101.html. Accessed 2/25/2019

2 *Science, Philosophy and Religion: a Symposium* by Albert Einstein, 1941

3 *"General Scholium," in Mathematical Principles of Natural Philosophy* by Isaac Newton, published 1729, 369.

4 www.osha.gov/pls/oshaweb/owadisp.show_document?p_id=25743&p_table=INTERPRETATIONS. Accessed 3/8/2019

5 Taken from *I Don't Have Enough Faith to Be an Atheist* by Norman Geisler and Frank Turek, © 2004 p. 102. Used by permission of Crossway, a publishing ministry of Good News Publishers. Wheaton, IL 60187, www.crossway.org

6 Taken from *I Don't Have Enough Faith to Be an Atheist* by Norman Geisler and Frank Turek, ©2004 p. 109. Used by permission of Crossway, a publishing ministry of Good News Publishers. Wheaton, IL 60187, www.crossway.org

7 Randall Niles with research taken from *It Couldn't Just Happen* by Lawrence O. Richards, ©1994, y Lawrence O. Richards. Used by permission of Thomas Nelson. www.thomasnelson.com, 139-140.

8 "The Origin of Life," in *Scientific American* by George Wald, ©1954 volume 191, Issue 2, 46

9 "The Just-so Universe: The Fine-Tuning of Constants and Conditions in the Cosmos," by Walter Bradley, in *Signs of Intelligence*, edited by William A. Demboski and James M. Kushiner ©2001 Brazos Press. Grand Rapids, MI 49301, 168.

10 "A Scientist Caught Between Two Faiths: Interview with Robert Jastrow" in *Christianity Today*, August 6, 1982, Vol. 26, Number 13; 15, 18.

Chapter 2

1 At the time of this writing.

2 *The Books and the Parchments* by F.F. Bruce ©1963, 3rd rev. ed.

3 Westwood NJ; Revell p. 178; The chart is taken from *A Ready Defense* by Josh McDowell, ©1992 by Josh McDowell. Used by permission of Thomas Nelson. www.thomasnelson.com , 44-45.

4 For more information, see *A Ready Defense*, 48-49. Taken from *A Ready Defense* by Josh McDowell, ©1992 by Josh McDowell. Used by permission of Thomas Nelson. www.thomasnelson.com

5 Also called the Merneptah Stele.

6 At the time of this writing.

7 *Alexander Duff* by Thomas Smith ©1883, Hadder & Stouten. London, UK, 36.

8 Retold several times on the internet.

9 or "God-breathed"

10 *The Moody Handbook of Theology* by Paul P. Enns ©2008, Chicago IL; Moody Publishers, 156.

Chapter 3

1 *Antiquities of the Jews* by Flavius Josephus

2 Taken from *The Case for the Resurrection of Jesus* © Copyright 2004 by Gary Habermas and Michael Licona. Published by Kregel Publications, Grand Rapids, MI. Used by permission of the publisher. All rights reserved. Chapter 9. And also taken from *I Don't Have Enough Faith to Be an Atheist* by Norman Geisler and Frank Turek, ©2004 p. 222. Used by permission of Crossway, a publishing ministry of Good News Publishers. Wheaton, IL 60187, www.crossway.org

3 Taken from *I Don't Have Enough Faith to Be an Atheist* by Norman Geisler and Frank Turek, © 2004 p. 223. Used by permission of Crossway, a publishing ministry of Good News Publishers. Wheaton, IL 60187, www.crossway.org

4 Some split history with the BCE/CE ("Common Era") labels. Even so, the birth of Jesus Christ has always been the dividing line in history.

5 Taken from *I Don't Have Enough Faith to Be an Atheist* by Norman Geisler and Frank Turek, © 2004 p. 269. Used by permission of Crossway, a publishing ministry of Good News Publishers. Wheaton, IL 60187, www.crossway.org

6 Quote and statistics from AllAboutGOD.com Ministries: www.AllAboutGOD.com (www.allaboutruth.org/messianic-prophecy-2.htm). Accessed 3/8/2019

7 The Father, the Son (Jesus), and the Holy Spirit are three Persons of the Trinity. The Persons are often called God the Father, God the Son, and God the Holy Spirit. In understanding this Trinity concept, some people like to make the analogy of ice, liquid, and steam all being water. While the doctrine (teaching) of the Trinity is much more complex, this analogy gives us a simple start to understanding this concept. We have additional Bible studies listed in our Resources section on Page 89 if you would like to learn more about each Person of the Trinity.

Chapter 4

1 *What Happened to me: Reflections of a Journey* by Randall Niles, What Happened to Me: Reflections of a Journey by Randall Niles, iUniverse, ©2004, 99. Excerpt from www.allaboutthejourney.org/what-is-faith.html. Accessed 2/25/2019

WORKS CITED

Books

Bradley, Walter. *The "Just So" Universe: The Fine-Tuning of Constants and Conditions of the Cosmos* in William Dembski and James Kushiner, eds., Signs of Intelligence. Grand Rapids: Brazos Press, 2001.

Bruce, F.F. *The Books and the Parchments*. Westwood: Revell, 1963.

Enns, Paul P. *Moody Handbook of Theology*. Chicago: Moody Press, 1989.

Geisler, Norman L. and Frank Turek. *I Don't Have Enough Faith to Be an Atheist*. Wheaton: Crossway Books, 2004.

Habermas, Gary and Michael R. Licona. *The Case for the Resurrection of Jesus*. Grand Rapids: Kregal Publications, 2004.

Josephus, Flavius. *Antiquities of the Jews*.

McDowell, Josh. *A Ready Defense*. Nashville: Thomas Nelson Publishers, 1993.

McDowell, Josh. *Evidence That Demands a Verdict*. Arrowhead Springs, CA: Campus Crusade for Christ, International, 1972.

Newton, Isaac. *The Mathematical Principles of Natural Philosophy*. trans. A. Motte. London, 1729.

Niles, Randall. *What Happened to Me: Reflections of a Journey*. iUniverse, 2004.

Richards, Lawrence O. *It Couldn't Just Happen*. Nashville: Thomas Nelson Publishers, 1994

Smith, Thomas. *Alexander Duff*. London: Hadder & Stouten, 1883.

Periodicals and other publications

Scientific American, "The Origin of Life," George Wald. August 1954.

Christianity Today, "A Scientist Caught Between Two Faiths: Interview with Robert Jastrow." August 6, 1982.

Einstein, Albert. *Science, Philosophy and Religion, A Symposium*, 1941.

Internet

www.AllAboutGOD.com

www.GotQuestions.org

www.osha.gov/pls/oshaweb/owadisp.show_document?p_id=25743&p_
    table=INTERPRETATIONS

WHO IS STONECROFT?

Every day, Stonecroft communicates the Gospel (the redemptive account of Jesus) in meaningful ways. Whether side-by-side with a neighbor or new friend or by a speaker sharing her transformational story, the Gospel of Jesus Christ goes forward. Stonecroft proclaims His love to women where they are, as they are through a variety of outreach experiences and small-group gatherings and Bible studies specifically designed for those not familiar with God. These are supported by online and print resources focused on sharing the compassionate message of Jesus.

For more than 80 years, Stonecroft volunteers have found ways to love women to Jesus Christ and equip them to share His Good News with others – always with a foundation of prayer and reliance on God.

Stonecroft understands and appreciates the influence of one woman's life. When you reach her, you touch everyone she knows – her family, friends, neighbors, and co-workers. The real truth of the Gospel brings real redemption into real lives.

Our life-changing, faith-building community resources include:

- Stonecroft Bible Studies

  We offer both topical and chapter-by-chapter studies. Stonecroft studies are designed for those in small groups to simply, yet profoundly, discover God's Word together.

- Conversations

  These thought-provoking, small-group resources engage women in conversation on topics that matter. *Conversations* include *Rest, Known, Enough*, and *Whole.*

- Outreach Experiences

  These set the stage for women to hear and share the Gospel with their communities. Whether in a large venue, workshop, or small group setting, Stonecroft women find ways to share the love of Christ.

- Stonecroft Military

  This specialized effort honors women connected to the U.S. military, whether servicewomen or military wives, and loves them to Jesus.

- stonecroft.org

    To learn more about Stonecroft, visit our website. Our site offers fresh content to equip and encourage you.

Dedicated and enthusiastic Stonecroft staff and volunteers serve together to inspire, equip, and encircle women as they share the love of Christ with the world. Your life matters. Join us today to become part of reaching your community with the Gospel of Jesus Christ. Become involved with Stonecroft.

For more information, contact:

Stonecroft
connections@stonecroft.org
800.525.8627
stonecroft.org

RESOURCES

Who is Jesus?

This small group experience helps you discover why Jesus came to earth and what He accomplished.

6 chapters

What is God Like?

God wants you to know Him, and that He pursues a relationship with you.

6 chapters

Who is the Holy Spirit?

Consider who the Holy Spirit is. Become more aware of God's activity in your life.

6 chapters

Rest

This conversation helps you discover how God enables us to find rest in an overly busy world.

4 conversations

Known

Achievements and appearance don't determine real worth. Instead, find love and acceptance in God's eyes.

4 conversations

Enough

God helps us embrace who we really are, rather than fear what we're missing.

4 conversations

Whole

God can heal our brokenness and shape us into the women He created us to be.

4 conversations

Go to stonecroft.org/store to check out these resources and other helpful titles.

ABOUT THE AUTHOR

 Internet missionary MeLissa Houdmann is co-founder along with her husband, Shea, of GotQuestions.org, one of the world's largest Christian online ministries helping people find answers about God and the Bible.

Following college, MeLissa served at Stonecroft with Lucille Sollenberger in the production of several celebrated Stonecroft Bible Studies. Valuable skills learned as Stonecroft employees empowered the Houdmanns to launch GotQuestions.org in 2002.

A prolific print media and web writer, MeLissa also currently serves as a Stonecroft Bible Studies coordinator in Colorado Springs, Colo. She is the original author of *Why Believe?* and is honored to submit this updated apologetics resource.

Stonecroft